fast and fresh

delicious and healthy family meals

First published in 2011

Parragon
Queen Street House
4 Queen Street
Bath
BA1 1HE UK

Copyright Parragon books Ltd 2011

ISBN: 978-1-4454-4049-1

Printed in China

The times given are an approximate guide only.
Preparation times differ according to the techniques used
by different people and the cooking times may also vary
from those given as a result of the type of oven used.
Optional ingredients, variations or serving suggestions
have not been included in the calculations.

Recipes using raw or very lightly cooked eggs should
be avoided by infants, the elderly, pregnant women
convalescents and anyone with a chronic condition.
Pregnant and breast-feeding women are advised to
avoid eating peanuts and peanut products. People with
nut allergies should be aware that some of the prepared
ingredients used in this book may contain nuts. Always
check the photography before use.

contents

introduction

In recent years, people have turned (or re-turned!) to the notion of using fresh, locally grown, ingredients to create the healthiest meals to serve their families and friends. In our busy worlds, we also want to be able to prepare these healthy meals as quickly as possible.

Fast & Fresh is a collection of recipes that focus on fresh ingredients, many of which are available at local farmers' markets, and are quick and easy to prepare. Here are fresh and easy appetizers, (*Shrimp Cocktail*), an assortment of salads, (*Waldorf Salad, Cobb Salad,* and *Southwest Corn Salad*), and a fascinating group of soups and stews, including (*Easy Gazpacho,* and *Spiced Pumpkin Soup*).

Of course, a broad selection of main dishes are included, from those featuring meat and fish, (*Ham Steaks with Carmelized Apples, Grilled Salmon Fillet with Fresh Mango Salsa,* and *Halibut Steaks with Spinach and Warm Bacon Dressing*) to hearty vegetable mains, and side dishes like *Succulent Succotash, Baked Spinach and Feta Frittata* and *Creamed Spinach.* Quick sweets using fresh ingredients complete the collection.

With a beautiful color photograph of each delectable recipe, this is a book every home cook will turn to for ideas for quick and easy meals made with the healthiest ingredients.

appetizers, snacks, and salads

shrimp cocktail

Unless you've cooked fresh shrimp at home, you've never really had a shrimp cocktail before.

serves 4-6

2 pounds jumbo shrimp (24-30 shrimp), deveined, but unpeeled

1 lemon cut in wedges

1 cup prepared cocktail sauce

For the poaching liquid

3 quarts cold water

½ onion, sliced

2 garlic cloves, peeled and bruised

2 springs tarragon

1 bay leaf

1 tablespoon Old Bay seasoning

½ lemon, juiced

1 teaspoon black peppercorns

For the cocktail sauce

½ cup ketchup

¼ cup chili sauce

¼ cup horseradish, or to taste

1 teaspoon fresh lemon juice

1 teaspoon Worcestershire sauce

Dash of hot sauce, optional

Pinch of salt

Frozen shrimp are now commonly available deveined (meaning the intestinal track removed), but with the shell on. This style makes the best shrimp cocktail since the shell adds flavor when they are poached.

If you can't find this type, get shell-on shrimp and use a pair of scissors to make a cut through the shell, down the back of the shrimp. Then use a small sharp knife to make $1/8$ inch deep incision and remove the intestinal track. Rinse under cold water.

Add all the poaching liquid ingredients to a large stockpot. Bring to a simmer over high heat. Turn the heat down to low and simmer for 30 minutes.

Fill a mixing bowl with ice water and set aside. Turn the heat under the poaching liquid to high, and bring to a boil. Add the shrimp and boil for 5 minutes or until cooked through. Transfer the shrimp into the ice water. When cold, drain well, and serve with cocktail sauce and lemon wedges.

For the cocktail sauce (makes 1 cup): Combine all the cocktail sauce ingredients in a small bowl, mix thoroughly, and refrigerate for at least one hour before serving.

guacamole

Guacamole, chips, and fresh salsa – the cornerstone of
any great party's snack table.

serves 12

6 ripe avocados, halved, pitted

4 green onions, light parts only, finely diced

1 jalapeno pepper, seeded, finely diced

1/3 cup chopped fresh cilantro

3 tbsps freshly squeezed lime juice

1½ tsp salt, or to taste

Cayenne to taste

Scoop the avocados into a bowl. Add the rest of the
ingredients and mash with a potato masher or fork as
smooth or chunky as you like. Best if chilled for 30 minutes
before serving.

clams casino

This is simply the best clam recipe ever. Whenever bacon and butter appear in the same recipe, you know you're in for a treat! Ironically, I've never eaten these in a casino.

makes 18

18 medium-sized (about 2½ inches) of littleneck clams

2 tbsps unsalted butter

3 strips center-cut bacon, each sliced into 6 equal pieces (18 total)

3 tbsps finely diced red bell pepper

3 garlic cloves, finely minced

⅓ cup plain breadcrumbs

1 tbsp finely grated Parmesan

⅛ tsp freshly ground black pepper

Pinch of salt

2 tbsps chopped flat leaf parsley

Lemon wedges

Rock salt as needed

Heat butter in a skillet over medium heat. Add the bacon and sauté until cooked, but not quite crisp. Using a slotted spoon, transfer the bacon to a plate and reserve.

Add the red pepper to the bacon drippings in the skillet, and cook for 2 minutes. Add the garlic and cook for 1 minute more. Turn off the heat and stir in the breadcrumbs, Parmesan, black pepper, and salt. Reserve the mixture until needed.

Add about 2 inches of water to a Dutch oven, or other heavy pot with a tight-fitting lid, and bring to a rapid boil over high heat. Add clams, cover, and cook for about 5 minutes, or just until the shells open. It's critical to remove and drain the clams as soon as they open. Allow the clams to cool until they can be handled.

Twist and pull the clamshells apart, and remove the clam. Place the clam back into the deeper of the two shell halves. Spread the rock salt on a heatproof baking dish, and set the clams on top of the salt, pressing in slightly.

Divide the breadcrumb mixture evenly over the top of each clamshell, and top with one piece of bacon. Broil on high, about 8 inches from the heat, until the tops are browned and the edges of the bacon are crisp. Sprinkle on the fresh parsley, and serve hot with lemon wedges.

easy gazpacho

This delicious cold soup is quick and easy to make, and hits the spot on a hot summer afternoon.

serves 4

1 small cucumber, peeled and chopped

2 red bell peppers, seeded, chopped

2 green bell peppers, seeded and chopped

2 garlic cloves, coarsely chopped

1 fresh basil sprig

2½ cups strained tomatoes

1 tablespoon extra-virgin olive oil

1 tablespoon red wine vinegar

1 tablespoon balsamic vinegar

1¼ cups vegetable stock

2 tablespoons lemon juice

Salt and pepper

For garnish

2 tablespoons peeled, diced cucumber

2 tablespoons finely chopped red onion

2 tablespoons seeded, finely chopped, red bell pepper

2 tablespoons seeded, finely chopped green bell pepper

Ice cubes

4 fresh basil sprigs

Put the cucumber, bell peppers, garlic, and basil in a food processor and process for 1½ minutes. Add the strained tomatoes, olive oil, and both kinds of vinegar and process until smooth.

Pour in the vegetable stock and lemon juice and stir. Transfer the mixture to a large bowl. Season to taste with salt and pepper. Cover with plastic wrap and let chill.

For the garnish: Prepare the cucumber, onion, and bell peppers, then place in small serving dishes or arrange decoratively on a plate. Place ice cubes in 4 large soup bowls. Stir the soup and ladle it into the bowls. Garnish with the basil sprigs and serve with the prepared vegetables and chunks of fresh crusty bread.

Note: The sweetness of basil works well with this soup, but cilantro is traditional and also delicious.

spiced pumpkin soup

Sure, pumpkin pie gets all the press, but this great gourd also makes a wonderful soup.

serves 4

2 (15-ounce) cans pumpkin puree

2 tablespoons olive oil

1 onion, chopped

1 garlic clove, chopped

1 tablespoon chopped fresh ginger

1 small red chile, seeded and finely chopped

2 tablespoons chopped fresh cilantro

1 bay leaf

2½ cups vegetable stock

Salt and pepper to taste

Light cream, to garnish

In a soup pot, heat the oil over medium heat. Add the onion and garlic and cook, stirring constantly, for about 4 minutes, or until slightly softened. Add the ginger, chile, cilantro, bay leaf, and pumpkin puree, and cook for 3 minutes.

Add the vegetable stock and bring to a boil. Reduce the heat and simmer gently, stirring occasionally, for 10 minutes. Remove from the heat, take out the bay leaf.

If you want the soup to be very smooth, transfer the soup to a food processor or blender and process until you reach the consistency you desire. Return the soup to the pan, and season to taste with salt and pepper.

Reheat gently, stirring. Remove from the heat, pour into warmed soup bowls, garnish each one with a swirl of cream, and serve.

waldorf salad

It's amazing how such a simple list of ingredients can come together to create such a delicious and complexly flavored salad. This sweet, crunchy classic is named for the Waldorf Astoria Hotel in New York City, where it was first created.

serves 6

¾ **cup raw walnut halves**

⅓ **cup mayonnaise**

2 **tablespoons freshly squeezed lemon juice**

1 **tablespoon plain yogurt**

½ **teaspoon salt**

Fresh ground black pepper to taste

3 **apples, cored, cut into 1-inch chunks**

1 **cup green or red seedless grape halves**

⅔ **cup sliced celery, about ¼-inch thick**

1 **small head butter lettuce**

Preheat oven to 350°F. Arrange walnuts on a baking sheet, and bake for 8 minutes. Let cool on a cutting board, roughly chop, and reserve.

Add the mayonnaise, lemon juice, yogurt, salt, and a few grinds of black pepper to a large mixing bowl. Whisk to combine thoroughly. Use a spatula to fold in the apples, grapes, celery, and walnuts. Mix until evenly coated with the dressing.

Lay down a few lettuce leaves on each plate and spoon the Waldorf salad over the top. Serve immediately.

Note: Use three different varieties of apple for an even more interesting salad.

three bean salad

Nothing says summer days more than a lovely light, bright green bean salad. This easy to make recipe is delicious and quick.

serves 4-6

6 oz mixed salad leaves, such as spinach, arrugala and frisée

1 red onion

3 oz radishes

6 oz cherry tomatoes

4 oz cooked beetroot

10 oz canned cannellini beans,
drained and rinsed

7 oz canned red kidney beans,
drained and rinsed

10½ oz canned flageolet beans,
drained and rinsed

1½ oz dried cranberries

2 oz roasted cashew nuts

8 oz feta cheese (drained weight), crumbled

For the dressing

4 tbsps extra virgin olive oil

1 tsp Dijon mustard

2 tbsps lemon juice

1 tbsp chopped fresh coriander

Salt and pepper

Thinly slice the onion, then cut in half to form half moons and put into a bowl.

Thinly slice the radishes, cut the tomatoes in half and peel the beetroot and add to the onion. Add all remaining ingredients with exception of the nuts and cheese.

To make the dressing, put all the ingredients into a screw-top jar and shake until well-blended.

Pour the dressing over the bean mixture, toss lightly, then spoon on top of the salad leaves. Scatter with the nuts and cheese and serve immediately.

potato and egg salad

If you find yourself at a summer picnic, and there isn't a big bowl of this salad there, leave immediately.

serves 6

4 lbs russet potatoes, peeled, quartered

3 hard-boiled eggs, chopped

1 cup diced celery

$1/3$ cup minced green onions,
white and light green parts only

$1\frac{1}{4}$ cup mayonnaise

2 tbsps cider vinegar

1 tbsp Dijon mustard

$1\frac{1}{2}$ tsps salt

$\frac{1}{2}$ tsp sugar

$\frac{1}{4}$ tsp freshly ground black pepper

$1/8$ tsp cayenne, optional

Boil potatoes in salted water until just tender, drain well, and let cool to room temperature. Cut into 1 inch pieces and add to a large bowl. Add the eggs and celery.

In a small mixing bowl combine the rest of the ingredients. Pour over the potato mixture, and use a spatula to thoroughly combine.

Chill in the refrigerator for at least one hour before serving.

caesar salad with garlic croutons

As the story goes, America's most popular restaurant salad was invented in 1924 by Caesar Cardini in Tijuana, Mexico. It's a masterpiece of taste and texture.

serves 12 small or 6 large

For the dressing

2 egg yolks, from coddled eggs

2 large garlic cloves, minced

3 whole anchovy fillets

¾ cup mayonnaise

½ cup finely grated Parmigiano-Reggiano Parmesan cheese

⅓ cup olive oil

¼ cup freshly squeezed lemon juice

1 tbsp cold water

1 tsp freshly ground black pepper, or to taste

Salt to taste

For the salads

6 hearts of romaine lettuce, torn or cut into
2 inch pieces, washed, dried thoroughly

¾ cup Caesar dressing, more as needed

4 cups Garlic Parmesan Croutons

1 cup shaved Parmesan cheese, more as needed

Freshly ground black pepper, to taste

For the dressing: To coddle eggs: Place 2 room temperature eggs in a small saucepan. Pour in boiling water until the eggs are covered. Leave for 1 minute, then drain and run under cold water until the eggs are cool enough to be handled. When cool separate the eggs and reserve the yolks.

Add the rest of the dressing ingredients to a blender, along with the egg yolks. Blend until smooth. Refrigerate until needed.

For the salads: Combine the romaine, croutons, and dressing in a large mixing bowl. Toss with tongs until the lettuce is completely coated with dressing. Divide onto chilled plates and top with the shaved Parmesan (a potato peeler works best for this), and freshly ground black pepper to taste. Serve immediately with extra dressing on the side. and garlic croutons.

cobb salad

America's most famous "composed" salad was invented at Los Angeles' Brown Derby restaurant in 1937. The ingredients are traditionally arranged in neat rows on top of the greens, but if you don't want to bother, it's just as delicious with everything tossed together.

serves 4

8 slices bacon

4 large handfuls mixed baby greens, or other lettuce, torn into bite-size pieces

3 hard-boiled eggs, peeled, chopped

4 cups cooked chicken, cubed

2 avocados, peeled, pitted, cubed

1 cup cherry tomatoes, halved

½ cup (about 4 ounces) crumbled Roquefort cheese

½ teaspoon Dijon mustard

¼ cup red wine vinegar

1 teaspoon Worcestershire sauce

1 clove garlic, crushed into a paste

¼ teaspoon salt

¼ teaspoon freshly ground black pepper

⅓ cup olive oil

Cook the bacon until crisp, drain on paper towels, and when cool enough to handle, crumble and set aside.

Arrange a bed of lettuce in shallow bowls. Arrange the eggs, bacon, chicken, avocados, tomatoes, and Roquefort cheese in rows on top of the lettuce, covering the surface completely.

In a bowl, whisk together the mustard, vinegar, Worcestershire, garlic, salt, and pepper. Slowly drizzle in the olive oil, whisking constantly, to form the dressing.

Drizzle the dressing evenly over the salad, and serve immediately.

southwest corn salad

This cool, colorful, and crunchy salad is perfect when fresh corn is in season, and you want to bring something fabulous to that summer cookout. Frozen corn may be used, but the salad just won't have that same sweet, crisp snap.

serves 6-8

3 tablespoons olive oil

3 cups fresh corn kernels, about 6 ears

1 (15 ounce) can black beans, well rinsed and drained

1 red bell pepper, seeded, diced

1 orange bell pepper, seeded, diced

1 jalapeño pepper, seeded, minced

4 thinly sliced green onions

1 clove garlic, crushed, minced

2 tablespoons chopped cilantro leaves

½ teaspoon ground cumin

¼ teaspoon chipotle pepper, or to taste

3 tablespoons fresh lime juice

1 tablespoon rice vinegar

1 teaspoon sugar

1 teaspoon salt

Heat the olive oil in a large nonstick pan over medium-high heat. Add the corn and sauté, stirring, for 3 to 4 minutes.

Turn off the pan and transfer corn into a large mixing bowl. Add the rest of the ingredients and toss to combine thoroughly.

Refrigerate before serving. Toss well, and taste and adjust for salt and spice before serving.

roasted red potato salad

Using red potatoes makes this salad both attractive and delicious. This salad looks so tasty, just dive right in.

serves 6

2½ pounds (8-10) small red potatoes, washed

Salt to taste

2 cloves garlic, finely minced

1 teaspoon Dijon mustard

Pinch of cayenne

¼ cup white wine vinegar

⅔ cup olive oil

Salt and freshly ground black pepper to taste

1 tablespoon chopped fresh Italian parsley

1 tablespoon chopped fresh tarragon

1 tablespoon chopped fresh chives

1 teaspoon minced fresh thyme leaves

Preheat oven to 400°F. Place the potatoes in a roasting pan. Bake for 25 to 30 minutes, or until tender (time will vary depending on size).

While the potatoes are in the oven, make the dressing. Add the garlic, mustard, cayenne, and vinegar to a large mixing bowl. Whisk in the oil, very slowly at first, in a steady stream until incorporated.

When the cooked potatoes are just cool enough to handle, cut in halves or quarters. Add and toss the warm potatoes in the dressing, along with salt and freshly ground black pepper to taste. Let sit for 15 minutes.
Add the herbs and toss again.

deli-style macaroni salad

Take your time, and use your sharpest knife to get a nice fine dice on the veggies in this classic pasta salad. When made right, this is a macaroni salad where every forkful bursts with flavor.

serves 8

1 pound dry elbow macaroni, cooked, rinsed in cold water, and drained well

For the dressing

1½ cups mayonnaise

½ cup sour cream

2 tablespoons cider vinegar

1 tablespoon Dijon mustard

1 teaspoon sugar

½ cup finely diced celery

¼ cup minced red onion

½ cup sweet pickle relish

¼ finely grated carrot

2 tablespoons seeded and finely diced red bell pepper

¼ cup chopped parsley

½ teaspoon freshly ground black pepper

1½ teaspoons salt, or to taste

Whisk together all the dressing ingredients in a large mixing bowl, and add the drained pasta. Toss to combine thoroughly.

Note: Some of the vegetables can be reserved to scatter over the top for a more colorful presentation.

quick main dishes

chicken fettuccini alfredo

This Italian-style favorite doesn't use butter, and replaces some of the traditional cream with chicken broth for a slightly lighter, but just-as-delicious version. Be sure to use real Parmigiano-Reggiano cheese, not the commercial, jarred cheese.

serves 4-6

2 cups low-sodium chicken broth

1½ pounds (2 large) skinless, boneless chicken breasts

2 cups heavy cream

4 cloves garlic, minced

2 large egg yolks

2 cups freshly grated Parmesan cheese

¼ cup chopped Italian parsley

Salt and freshly ground black pepper to taste

1 pound fettuccini

Bring the broth to a simmer in a saucepan over medium heat then add the chicken. Cover, reduce the heat to low and simmer for 12 minutes. Turn off the heat and let the chicken sit in the hot broth for 15 minutes. When the chicken has cooled, remove from the broth, cut into thin slices and reserve.

Put the pasta water on to boil. Bring the chicken broth back to a boil over high heat. Cook until the broth has reduced by half. Add the cream and garlic and when the mixture comes to a simmer, reduce the heat to low.

Beat the egg yolks in a small bowl. Slowly whisk in a half cup of the hot cream mixture to warm the egg yolks. Turn off the heat and whisk the egg mixture into the cream sauce. Stir in 1 cup of the Parmesan cheese, and the parsley. Season with salt and freshly ground black pepper to taste. Stir in the sliced chicken. Cover and reserve.

Boil the fettuccini in salted water according to directions. Drain well, but do not rinse. Quickly return the hot pasta to the pot, and pour over the sauce. Stir well with a wooden spoon, cover, and let sit 1 minute. Remove the cover, stir in the last cup of the Parmesan cheese, and let sit for one more minute. Serve hot topped with additional grated Parmesan cheese.

Note: In the summer replace the parsley with some nice fresh basil.

spiced-rubbed seared tuna steaks with balsamic reduction

These seared-on-the-outside, rare-in-the-middle tuna steaks are very popular these days, and quite easy to make at home. The sharp, intensively flavored balsamic reduction is a perfect foil for the buttery texture and rich, meaty taste of the tuna.

serves 4

1½ pounds center-cut Ahi tuna fillet

1½ teaspoons kosher salt

1 teaspoon ground coriander

1 teaspoon paprika

¼ teaspoon cayenne pepper

1½ tablespoons coarse freshly ground black pepper

2 tablespoons vegetable oil

4 lemon wedges, garnish

For the reduction

6 tablespoons aged balsamic vinegar

1 lemon, juiced

1 garlic clove, peeled, halved

To make the reduction: Place the balsamic vinegar, lemon juice, and garlic in a small saucepan on the stove over medium-low heat. Simmer until the mixture reduces by half. Turn off the heat and reserve until needed. This sauce does not have to be hot. The reduction will thicken slightly as it cools.

Slice the tuna fillet into 4 equal-size rectangular steaks. In a small bowl, combine the salt, coriander, paprika, and cayenne. Lay the tuna steaks out on a plate, and sprinkle the spice mixture evenly on all sides.

Evenly coat the tuna steaks with the freshly ground black pepper, and gently press it in, so that it adheres to the surface, being careful not to smash the flesh.

Place a thick-bottomed frying pan or cast iron skillet on the stove over medium-high heat. Add the oil and swirl to coat the pan. When small wisps of smoke appear, add the tuna to the pan and sear the steaks for about 1 minute per side, or until desired doneness is reached. Remove to a cutting board.

For presentation, cut each steak diagonally into 4 to 5 slices and fan on a plate. Serve with a small amount of sauce drizzled along side. Garnish with lemon wedges if desired.

turkey cutlets

These crispy cutlets are fast to make, and addictive to eat. A squeeze of fresh lemon is all you need for flavor, but these work nicely with gravy, tartar sauce, or even barbecue sauce.

serves 4-6

1½ cups all-purpose flour

1 teaspoon garlic powder

1 teaspoon onion powder

¼ teaspoon cayenne pepper

4 large eggs

4 cups Japanese-style panko breadcrumbs, or more as needed

2 pounds turkey cutlets, sliced or pounded to an even ¼ inch thickness

Salt and freshly ground black pepper, to taste

1 teaspoon poultry seasoning

Vegetable oil for frying

Lemon wedges

Place the flour, garlic powder, onion powder, and cayenne in a shallow dish. Stir thoroughly to combine; reserve. Whisk the eggs in a mixing bowl; reserve. Pour the breadcrumbs into a shallow baking dish; reserve.

Season the turkey cutlets on both sides generously with the salt and freshly ground black pepper to taste, and dust lightly with the poultry seasoning.

Dredge the turkey cutlets in the seasoned flour. One or two at a time, dip the cutlets into the egg, and once coated, transfer into the breadcrumbs. Turn over several times, pressing lightly in the crumbs to make sure the meat is thoroughly coated. Transfer cutlets to a pan, and continue until they're all breaded. When done breading, let rest for 15 minutes before frying.

Pour about ¼ inch of oil into a large, heavy skillet (ideally cast iron) and set over medium-high heat. When the oil is hot enough to fry (350°F. or test with a small piece of bread), cook for about 2 to 3 minutes per side, or until golden brown and cooked through.

Work in batches, drain on paper towels or wire rack, and keep in a warm oven (175°F.) until all are done. Serve immediately with lemon wedges, or other sauce of your choice.

grilled salmon fillet
with fresh mango salsa

Mango salsa is a delicious accompaniment to grilled salmon, and it so easy to make well. The tropical and tangy topping is a perfect match with smoky fish.

serves 6

6 (7 ounce) salmon fillets, boneless and skinless

2 teaspoons kosher salt

2 teaspoons vegetable oil

For the mango salsa

1 ripe mango, peeled, seeded, and diced small (about 1½ cups)

2 tablespoons red bell pepper, finely diced

2 tablespoons red onion, diced

1 tablespoon jalapeño, minced

2 tablespoons fresh lime juice

2 tablespoons chopped fresh cilantro

1 tablespoon rice vinegar

1 tablespoon olive oil

¼ teaspoon cumin

Pinch of cayenne pepper, optional

Salt to taste

Lime wedges to garnish

To make the mango salsa: In a mixing bowl, combine all the mango salsa ingredients and set aside. Let sit out at room temperature for 30 minutes before serving. Toss before using.

Brush the salmon lightly with the vegetable oil, and season generously on all sides with the salt. Preheat grill to medium-high. Grill the salmon for 5 to 7 minutes per side until lightly charred, and cooked to your desired doneness. Serve with the mango salsa, lime wedges, and salt.

ham steaks with carmelized apples

Applesauce is a natural with ham, but when you use freshly sautéed apple slices it becomes a very special experience.

serves 4-6

¼ cup firmly packed light brown sugar

1 tablespoon apple cider vinegar

1 cup apple cider or juice

Small pinch of cinnamon

2 teaspoons Dijon mustard

4 firm apples (Granny Smith, or any good cooking apple), peeled, cored, cut into quarters, and then each quarter into 4 slices

3 tablespoons unsalted butter, divided

Salt and freshly ground black pepper to taste

2 pounds ham steaks, cut into serving size pieces, or freshly baked ham slices

In a small bowl, whisk together the brown sugar, cider vinegar, apple cider or juice, cinnamon, and Dijon mustard. Reserve until needed. Prep the apples as directed.

Melt 2 tablespoons of the butter in a large skillet over high heat. As soon as the butter melts, wait half a minute and add the apples. Sauté for 3 to 4 minutes, or until the edges start to brown slightly.

Pour in the reserved sugar/vinegar mixture, turn the heat down to medium-high, and cook until the apples are tender and the liquid has reduced down to a glaze. If the liquid begins to get too thick before the apples are tender, just add a splash of water and continue cooking.

Taste and season with salt and freshly ground black pepper to taste. It may seem odd to add salt and black pepper to an apple sauce, but it's a very important flavor component.

Melt 1 tablespoon of butter in the skillet, and gently warm the ham steaks over medium-low heat. Remember, the ham is already cooked, so you just want it warmed up, not re-cooked. Serve with the hot apples spooned over the top.

halibut steaks with spinach and warm bacon dressing

A warm spinach salad with the traditional, sweet-and-sour bacon dressing is always a special treat, but it also makes a great bed for pan-grilled halibut.

serves 4

4 (6 ounce) halibut steaks or fillets

2 teaspoons vegetable oil

Salt and freshly ground black pepper to taste

4 handfuls (about 12 ounces) baby spinach, washed and dried

½ cup cherry tomato halves

4 lemon wedges

For the dressing

1 tablespoon olive oil

4 strips bacon, cut in small pieces

½ cup cider vinegar

4 teaspoon sugar

2 teaspoons lemon juice

½ teaspoon dry mustard

$1/8$ teaspoon freshly ground black pepper

Pinch of salt

To make the dressing: Add the olive oil to a saucepan and cook the bacon over medium heat until crisp. Turn off the heat. Remove and reserve the bacon pieces, leaving the fat in the pan. Whisk in the rest of the dressing ingredients, and reserve. The dressing does not have to be emulsified, as it will be brought to a boil before serving.

Brush the halibut with the vegetable oil and season generously with salt and freshly ground black pepper. Preheat a cast iron pan over medium-high heat, and grill the halibut for about 4 minutes per side, or until the desired doneness is reached.

While the halibut is cooking, add the spinach and cherry tomatoes to a large mixing bowl. When the fish is close to being done, bring the dressing to a boil, whisking, and pour over the spinach. Toss until the leaves are evenly coated and slightly wilted. Divide onto four plates.

Top with the cooked halibut. Finish with the reserved crisp bacon and a wedge of lemon.

Note: This is also wonderful with salmon, and if you like, thinly sliced mushrooms can be added to the spinach.

baked spinach and feta frittata

You could use frozen, but with large bags of fresh, prewashed and picked spinach so readily available in stores, why would you?

serves 6

1 pound fresh spinach leaves, washed

1 tablespoon butter

6 slices bacon, cut in ¼ inch pieces

½ onion, diced

12 eggs, beaten

Salt and freshly ground black pepper to taste

Pinch of cayenne pepper

½ cup (3-4 ounces) crumbled feta cheese

Preheat oven to 350°F. Put a large stockpot over high heat. Add the butter, and as soon as it melts, dump in all the spinach and cover the pot quickly. Leave for one minute, uncover, and continue cooking, stirring the spinach with a long wooden spoon, until just wilted. Transfer to a colander to drain. When the spinach is cool enough to handle, squeeze as much liquid out as possible, and roughly chop. Reserve until needed.

In a 10- to 12-inch ovenproof skillet, cook the bacon over medium heat until almost crisp, add the onions and a pinch of salt, and continue cooking until the onions are translucent, 6 to 7 minutes. Any excess bacon fat can be removed at this point.

Stir in the spinach. Season with salt, freshly ground black pepper, and cayenne to taste. When the spinach is heated through, add the eggs and stir with a spatula to combine thoroughly. Turn off the heat, and top with the crumbled feta cheese. Use the spatula to press the cheese down into the egg slightly.

Bake for 10 minutes, then finish under the broiler for about 3 minutes, or until the eggs are just set, and the top is lightly browned. Let rest for 5 to 10 minutes before slicing and serving.

grilled lamb chops with orange mint jelly

These lamb rib chops are too gorgeous to cover in that bright green mint jelly from the supermarket. Making your own orange mint sauce is very easy, and so much better tasting.

serves 6

3 cloves garlic, minced

2 tbsps olive oil

1 tsp cumin

½ tsp ground coriander

½ tsp black pepper

⅛ tsp cinnamon

½ tsp dried rosemary, crushed

½ tsp dried thyme

16 lamb rib chops (about 2½ lbs)

Salt to taste

For the mint sauce

½ cup orange marmalade or jelly

1 tbsp rice wine vinegar

1 tbsp water

2 tbsps freshly chopped mint

¼ tsp red pepper flakes, optional

Pinch of salt

In a large baking dish, combine all the ingredients, except for the lamb chops and salt. Mix until combined, add the lamb chops and rub the marinade into both sides. Cover and refrigerate for 30 minutes. Lamb chops may be marinated over night for a stronger flavor.

Combine all the sauce ingredients in a small mixing bowl. Refrigerate until needed.

Pre-heat grill, grill pan, or broiler. Remove chops from marinade and salt both sides generously. Cook about 3 minutes per side for medium-rare, or until desired doneness has been reached. Let rest for 5 minutes before serving with the mint sauce.

beef tenderloin with peppercorn sauce

This steakhouse classic has been modified for the home kitchen, and makes a great choice for that next "fancy" special occasion dinner.

serves 4

4 (8 ounce) center-cut beef tenderloin filet mignon steaks

Salt to taste

Coarsely ground whole black peppercorns

2 tablespoons clarified butter, procedure below

2 tablespoons minced shallots

½ cup brandy

1 cup veal stock or low-sodium beef broth

⅓ cup heavy cream

½ teaspoon Dijon mustard

3 drops Worcestershire sauce

1 tablespoon cold unsalted butter

Salt the steaks generously on both sides. Set your pepper grinder to a coarse setting and very generously coat both sides of the steaks with pepper. (You can also crush the peppercorns with the bottom of a heavy pot or skillet.)

To clarify the butter: melt some butter and allow it to sit until the oils separate from the milk solids and water. Skim the milky foam from the surface and pour off the clarified butter being careful to not add the water at the bottom.

Add 2 tablespoons of clarified butter to a large, heavy skillet. Place over high flame until very hot. Add the steaks and cook over medium-high heat for about 4 minutes per side for medium-rare, or until desired doneness. Tranfer to a plate and cover loosely with foil.

Turn off the flame and deglaze the skillet with the brandy. Turn the heat back on high, and as soon as the brandy is almost evaporated, stir in the cream, veal stock, mustard, and Worcestershire sauce, scraping the bottom of the skillet with a whisk to dissolve any meat juices caramelized on the bottom. Boil for a few minutes to reduce by half. Turn off the heat and whisk in the cold butter. Taste and adjust seasoning.

Place the steaks back in the hot sauce, tossing to coat. Serve immediately.

drunken mussels

This is probably the easiest shellfish recipe ever. The mussels are quickly steamed in an aromatic wine broth, and in minutes you're ready to enjoy. Be sure to have some grilled bread around so as not to waste any of the delicious juices.

serves 4 large portions or 6 small portions

4 tbsps butter

4 cloves garlic, sliced thin

1 shallot, thinly sliced

1½ cups white wine

¼ cup chopped fresh Italian parsley

½ tbsp lemon zest

Pinch of red pepper flakes, optional

3 lbs fresh mussels, scrubbed and rinsed

Lemon wedges, optional

Add the butter to a large stockpot (one with a tight-fitting lid). Melt it over medium heat, and add the garlic and shallots; cook for one minute, or until they begin to sizzle.

Add the wine, parsley, lemon zest, and pepper flakes. Turn the heat to high and bring the mixture to a boil. Add the mussels and cover quickly. Cook for 3 minutes, give the pot a little shake back and forth, and cook for another 2 to 4 minutes, or until the mussels have opened.

As soon as the shells open, serve immediately. The mussels will shrivel up to nothing if left to simmer in the hot liquid. Divide among some deep bowls. Taste the broth for salt (usually the mussels provide enough natural salt, but add some if needed). Ladle some of the broth over each bowl, and dig in. Serve with extra lemon wedges if desired.

garlic shrimp angel hair

Angel hair pasta is perfect for soaking up this very light, but very garlicky sauce. Together they make a great base for the sweet, freshly sautéed shrimp.

serves 6

2 lbs raw, peeled and deveined shrimp, shells reserved

3 tbsps butter

3 cups water

¼ cup olive oil

Salt to taste

¼ cup freshly minced garlic

½ cup diced tomatoes

½ cup cream

1 lemon, juiced

¼ tsp red chili flakes, or to taste

3 tbsps chopped Italian parsley

1 (14 oz) package dry angel hair pasta

6 lemon wedges, optional

To make the shrimp stock: Place the shrimp shells in a saucepan, along with 1 tbsp of butter, and place over medium heat. Sauté the shells for about 4 minutes, then add 3 cups of water. Bring to a simmer, reduce heat to low, and simmer for 15 minutes. Strain and reserve stock. Place a pot of salted water on to boil for the pasta.

Add the olive oil to a large skillet over high heat. Season the shrimp with salt. As soon as the oil in the pan is hot and begins to shimmer, add the shrimp and sauté for 3 to 4 minutes, until they just turn pink. Remove to a bowl with a slotted spoon, leaving the olive oil in the pan.

Add 2 tbsps of butter to the skillet and sauté the garlic over medium-low heat for about 2 minutes. Do not brown the garlic. Add the tomatoes, shrimp stock, and cream. Turn the heat to high, and bring the mixture to a boil, scraping the bottom with a wooden spoon to release any caramelized bits. Cook until reduced by half, about 10 minutes.

Cook the angel hair pasta 1 minute less than the package states. Drain into a colander. While the pasta is draining, add the shrimp to the sauce, along with the lemon juice, chili flakes, and parsley. Transfer the pasta back into the pot, and pour over the shrimp and sauce. Stir to combine, and let sit for one minute to absorb the sauce. Taste for salt, and then use tongs to divide the angel hair between the 6 plates.

smothered pork chops

This southern classic features pan-fried pork chops covered in a simple, but super savory onion gravy. These are great over rice, which helps soak up the delicious gravy.

serves 4

4 large pork chops, about 1½-inch thick

1 teaspoon poultry seasoning

Salt and freshly ground black pepper to taste

2 tablespoons vegetable oil

1 tablespoon butter

1 large yellow onion, sliced

4 cloves garlic, finely minced

1 tablespoon flour

1½ cups chicken broth

¼ cup buttermilk

¼ cup water

Season pork chops on both sides with the poultry seasoning, salt, and pepper. Heat the oil in a large frying pan over medium-high flame. When the oil is hot, brown the pork chops well, about 5 minutes per side. Remove from the pan and reserve on a plate.

Pour off the excess oil, and place the pan back on the stove over medium heat. Add the butter and the onions, along with a big pinch of salt. Sauté for about 10 minutes, or until the onions are well-browned. The onions need to caramelize for best results.

Stir in the garlic and cook for 1 minute. Stir in the flour and cook for 2 minutes. Add the chicken broth, buttermilk, and water. As the mixture comes to a simmer, use a wooden spoon to scrape any browned bits from the bottom of the pan.

Turn the heat to low, and let the onion gravy gently simmer for 15 minutes. Add a splash of water if it seems to be getting too thick. Add the pork chops and any juices back into the pan, and coat with the gravy. Cook for about 10 minutes, or until the pork reaches your desired level of doneness. Taste for seasoning and adjust, if necessary. Serve pork chops over rice, topped with the onion gravy.

broiled rainbow trout with lemon parsley brown butter

One of the simplest of all seafood accompaniments, this classic brown butter sauce is perfect with mild-flavored trout.

serves 6

6 tablespoons unsalted butter

6 whole boneless rainbow trout

Salt and freshly ground black pepper to taste

3 tablespoons fresh lemon juice

¼ cup chopped fresh parsley

Lemon wedges to garnish

Place the butter in a saucepan over medium-low heat. Cook until the butter turns a golden brown color, and takes on a nutty aroma. Reduce heat to very low and keep warm.

Remove the heads from the trout, and place skin-side-down on lightly-greased foil-lined baking sheets. Lightly brush a little of the browned butter over the surface. Season generously with salt and fresh ground black pepper.

Broil about 4 inches from the flame for 3 to 5 minutes, or until fish flakes when tested with a fork. While the fish is cooking, turn the butter up to medium heat and whisk in the lemon juice. As soon as the mixture comes to a boil, add the parsley, turn off the heat.

When ready, serve the trout on warm plates with the hot lemon parsley brown butter spooned over the top. Serve lemon wedges on the side.

oyster po' boys

Fried oysters are one of the most traditional fillings of this New Orleans classic. Once you choose your filling, you just have to decide if you want it "undressed" (plain) or "dressed" (with lettuce, tomatoes, and mayonnaise), as in this recipe.

serves 6

Generous ¼ cup yellow cornmeal

⅓ cup all-purpose flour

Pinch of cayenne

24 fresh live oysters

Vegetable oil, for deep-frying

1 French baguette

Hot pepper sauce, to taste (optional)

2 dill pickles, sliced (optional)

Mayonnaise

4 tomatoes, sliced

Shredded iceberg lettuce

Salt and pepper

Put the cornmeal, flour, cayenne, and salt and pepper to taste into a plastic bag, hold closed, and shake to mix. Shuck the oysters, running an oyster knife under each oyster to loosen it from its shell. Pour off the liquor. Add the oysters to the bag and shake until well coated.

Heat at least 2 inches of oil in the largest skillet you have over high heat until the temperature reaches 350°F to 375°F, or until a cube of bread browns in 30 seconds. Add as many oysters as will fit without overcrowding and fry for 2 to 3 minutes until the coating is crisp and lightly browned. Remove the oysters from the oil with a slotted spoon and drain on paper towels. Reheat the oil, then cook the remaining oysters.

Cut the baguette in half, without cutting all the way through. Open the bread out like a book and use a spoon to scoop out the crumbs from the bottom half, leaving a border all around the edge.

Spread mayonnaise over the top and bottom halves. Lay the oysters all along the length. Sprinkle with hot pepper sauce to taste and dill pickles, if using. Dress with tomato slices all along the length, then add the shredded lettuce. Close the sandwich and cut into 4 equal portions and wrap in paper napkins to serve.

delicious sides

asparagus with lemon butter sauce

It's not really Spring until you see bright green
plates of asparagus on the table.

serves 4

**2 lbs asparagus spears,
trimmed**

1 tbsp olive oil

Salt and pepper

For the sauce

Juice of 1 lemon

2 tbsps water

1 stick butter cut into cubes

Pre-heat oven to 400°F.

Lay the asparagus spears out in a single layer on a large
baking sheet. Drizzle over the oil, season to taste with salt
and pepper and roast in the pre-heated oven for 10 minutes,
or until just tender.

Meanwhile, make the sauce. Pour the lemon juice into a
saucepan and add the water. Heat for a minute or so, then
slowly add the butter, cube by cube, stirring constantly until
it has all been incorporated.

Season to taste with pepper and serve immediately, drizzled
over the asparagus.

braised red cabbage & apples

Red cabbage absorbs new flavors extremely well, and the addition of the vinegar makes this a delicious side dish.

serves 6

- 1 tsp of whole caraway seeds
- 1 tbsp vegetable oil
- 1 red onion, halved and thinly sliced
- 2 tbsps brown sugar
- 1 small red cabbage, shredded
- 2 apples, peeled and thinly sliced
- 2 tbsps red wine
- ½ cup apple juice
- 2 tbsps cider vinegar
- Salt and freshly ground black pepper
- 1 tsp lemon juice

In a saucepan over medium heat, dry roast the caraway seeds for about 1 minute until they start to give off an aroma.

Heat the oil in a large pot over medium heat, add the onion, and sauté for 5 minutes until it becomes translucent. Add the brown sugar, stir, and add the cabbage and apples. Stir for a few minutes until the cabbage wilts. Add in the red wine, apple juice, and vinegar. Add the toasted caraway seeds and salt and pepper to taste. Bring the mixture to a boil, lower to a simmer, add the lemon juice, cover, and cook for 30 minutes.

Note: Braised cabbage is wonderful served with chicken, meat, or pork dishes.

succulent succotash

This is a modern take on a very old Native American staple, and makes a great, colorful side dish for almost any meal.

serves 8

1 tbsp olive oil

½ tbsp butter

½ yellow onion, diced

3 garlic cloves, minced

1 jalapeno or other small hot chile pepper, sliced

½ red bell pepper, diced

½ cup diced tomatoes, fresh if available

4 oz green beans, cut in ½ inch pieces

1½ cups fresh or frozen corn

1 cup frozen baby lima beans, thawed

1 cup cubed green zucchini

½ tsp ground cumin

Pinch of cayenne

¼ cup water

Salt and freshly ground black pepper to taste

Place a large skillet on medium heat, and add the olive oil and butter. When the butter foams up, add the onions and a big pinch of salt. Sauté for about 5 minutes, or until the onions begin to soften and turn golden.

Add the garlic, jalapeno, and bell pepper; sauté for 3 minutes. Add the rest of the ingredients, and cook, stirring occasionally until the vegetables are tender. More liquid may be added if the mixture gets too dry. When done, taste for salt, and adjust the seasoning if needed. Serve immediately.

classic cole slaw

This very simple cole slaw is a great all-purpose recipe for any picnic or barbecue.

serves 12

2 lbs thinly sliced green cabbage

2 carrots, peeled, grated or finely julienned on a vegetable slicer

½ cup pineapple juice

1 cup mayonnaise

2 tsps sugar

¼ tsp cayenne pepper, or to taste

Salt and fresh ground black pepper to taste

Place the cabbage and carrot in a large mixing bowl. In a smaller bowl, whisk together the rest of the ingredients. Taste and adjust the sweetness and spiciness if so desired. Pour over the cabbage mixture and toss until coated.

Best if dressed within 30 minutes of serving, so it stays crisp and fresh.

Taste for seasoning and toss again right before serving.

steakhouse creamed spinach

This is the king of the steakhouse side dishes. It's not a real steak dinner unless there's creamed spinach on the table.

serves 4-6

½ cup unsalted butter

24 oz pre-washed, ready-to-use baby spinach

½ onion, finely diced

1 whole clove

3 cloves garlic, very finely minced

⅓ cup flour

1½ cups cold milk

Pinch freshly ground nutmeg

Salt and pepper, to taste

Put a large stockpot over high heat. Add 1 tbsp of the butter, and as soon as it melts, dump in all the spinach and cover quickly. Leave for one minute, uncover, and continue cooking, stirring the spinach with a long wooden spoon, until just barely wilted. Transfer to a colander to drain.

When the spinach is cool enough to handle, squeeze as much liquid out as possible, and roughly chop. Press between paper towels to draw out the last of the water, and reserve until needed.

Melt the rest of the butter in a saucepan over medium heat. Add the onions and cook for about 5 minutes, or until translucent. Whisk in the flour and cook for 3 minutes, stirring. Add the garlic and cook for 1 minute. Pour in the cold milk, whisking constantly, and cook until it comes to a simmer. Reduce heat to low and simmer for another 5 minutes. The sauce will thicken as it cooks.

Season the sauce with nutmeg, salt and fresh ground black pepper to taste. Add the spinach, and stir to combine. The dish is ready to serve as soon as the spinach is heated through. Taste once more, and adjust seasoning before serving.

perfect mashed potatoes

Almost everyone loves smooth, creamy mashed potatoes. But they have to be smooth and creamy, not lumpy. A potato masher is invaluable but a potato ricer is preferable because it presses the potato through tiny holes and makes fine 'worms' which means you never get lumps.

serves 4

2 pounds (5-6 medium) starchy potatoes, such as Idaho potatoes

4 tablespoons (½ stick) butter

3 tablespoons milk

Salt and freshly ground pepper

Peel the potatoes, placing them in cold water as you prepare the others to prevent them from going brown.

Cut the potatoes into even-sized chunks and cook in a large saucepan of boiling salted water over a medium heat, covered, for 20 to 25 minutes until they are tender. Test with the point of a knife, but make sure you test right to the middle to avoid lumps.

Remove the pan from the heat and drain the potatoes. Return the potatoes to the hot pan and mash with a potato masher until smooth.

Add the butter and continue to mash until it is all mixed in, then add the milk.

Taste the mash and season with salt and pepper to taste. Serve at once.

Variations: For herb mash, mix in 3 tablespoons chopped fresh parsley, thyme or mint. For mustard or horseradish mash, mix in 2 tablespoons wholegrain mustard or horseradish sauce. For pesto mash, stir in 4 tablespoons fresh pesto, and for nutmeg mash, grate ½ a nutmeg into the mash and add ½ cup plain yogurt. To make creamed potato, add ½ cup sour cream and 2 tablespoons snipped fresh chives.

naughty but nice sweet treats

chocolate chip cookies

A well-made chocolate chip cookie is about as close to perfection as you'll ever get.

makes 30 cookies

2¼ cups all-purpose flour

1 teaspoon baking soda

1 teaspoon salt

1 cup (2 sticks) butter, room temperature

¾ cup firmly packed light brown sugar

¾ cup sugar

1 teaspoon vanilla extract

2 large eggs

2 cups semisweet chocolate chips

1 cup chopped walnuts, optional

Preheat oven to 375°F. Add the flour, baking soda, and salt to a small mixing bowl. Whisk together briefly to combine. In another bowl, use an electric mixer to beat the butter, brown sugar, white granulated sugar, and vanilla extract until light and creamy.

Add eggs one at a time, beating thoroughly after each addition. Stir in the flour mixture until combined. Stir in the chocolate chips and nuts, if using. Drop the cookie dough by rounded tablespoons on ungreased baking sheets about 3 inches apart.

Bake for about 10 minutes, or until lightly browned around the edges. Let sit on the baking sheets for 2 minutes, and then remove to wire cooling racks.

peanut butter cookies

You know that feeling when you're really craving "something" good, but can't decide what that "something" is? It's these melt-in-your-mouth peanut butter cookies.

makes 12-15 cookies

1½ cups all-purpose flour

½ teaspoon baking powder

½ teaspoon salt

1 cup creamy peanut butter

½ cup (1 stick) butter, room temperature

1¼ teaspoons vanilla extract

½ cup firmly packed light brown sugar

½ cup sugar

2 eggs

Preheat oven to 350°F. Sift together the flour, baking powder, and salt in a mixing bowl; reserve. In a large mixing bowl, cream the peanut butter, butter, and vanilla together until smooth. Add the sugars, and cream for one more minute. Mix in the eggs one at a time. Mix in the flour, half at a time.

Wrap the dough in plastic wrap and refrigerate for at least 2 hours. Once chilled, roll or scoop the dough into 1½-inch balls, and place 3 inches apart on an ungreased or silicon-lined baking sheet.

Use a fork to flatten each ball by making a crisscross pattern. Bake for 15 minutes or until golden. Remove cookies from oven, and let cool on the baking sheet for 5 minutes. Transfer to a cooling rack with a spatula, and allow to cool to at least warm before serving.

chocolate walnut fudge

Contrary to what you might have heard, chocolate fudge is not hard to make. This easy recipe produces rich, smooth fudge every time.

makes 36 pieces

1½ cups sugar

1 (7-ounce) jar marshmallow crème

²/₃ cup evaporated milk

3 tablespoons butter

¼ teaspoon salt

1½ cups milk chocolate chips

1½ cups semisweet chocolate chips

½ cup chopped walnuts, optional

1 teaspoon vanilla extract

2 teaspoons cocoa, optional

Line an 8x8-inch pan with foil, and set aside. Add the sugar, marshmallow crème, evaporated milk, butter, and salt to a large, heavy-bottomed saucepan; place over medium heat. Cook, stirring, until the mixture begins to boil. When it begins to boil, set a timer for exactly 6 minutes. Stir constantly until the timer rings.

Turn off heat, and add in the chocolate chips. Stir until the chocolate is melted, then add the walnuts and vanilla. Pour into the pan, and spread evenly. Cover and refrigerate until firm. Dust with cocoa if desired, cut into 36 squares.

blueberry muffins

The sour cream gives these blueberry muffins a nice
richness, and keeps them moist and tender.

makes 16 muffins

3 cups all-purpose flour

¾ teaspoon salt

1 tablespoon baking powder

½ teaspoon baking soda

1 cup sugar

½ cup (1 stick) butter, softened

finely grated zest from one lemon

2 tablespoons vegetable oil

2 large eggs

1 cup sour cream

½ cup milk

½ teaspoon lemon extract, optional

2 cups fresh blueberries

Preheat oven to 375°F. Sift together the flour, salt, baking powder, and baking soda into a bowl; reserve.

In a large mixing bowl, beat the sugar, butter, lemon zest, and vegetable oil until light and creamy. Beat in the eggs one at a time. Whisk in the sour cream, milk, and lemon extract.

Add half the dry ingredients, and stir until just barely combined. Add the remaining dry ingredients, along with the blueberries, and fold with a spatula until just combined.

Line the muffin tins with paper baking cups. Fill each to the top with batter. Bake for 30 minutes to a beautiful golden brown. When cool enough to handle, remove muffins from the tins and serve.

lemon poppy seed muffins

Imagine a day you are so busy you miss breakfast, and have to settle for grabbing a lemon poppy seed muffin on the way out. That is a pretty good morning!

makes 12 muffins

2 cups all-purpose flour

½ teaspoon salt

1½ teaspoons baking powder

¼ teaspoon baking soda

½ cup (1 stick) unsalted butter, softened

1 cup sugar

Finely grated zest from 2 lemons

2 large eggs

2 tablespoons lemon juice

1 cup sour cream

2 tablespoons poppy seeds

For the glaze

1 tablespoon lemon juice

3 tablespoons confectioners' sugar

Preheat oven to 350°F. Whisk together the flour, salt, baking powder, and baking soda in a bowl, and reserve until needed.

In a mixing bowl, beat the butter, sugar, and lemon zest, until light and creamy. Beat in the eggs one at a time, mixing thoroughly before adding the next. Stir in a third of the flour mixture until just combined. Stir in the lemon juice, and half of the sour cream until combined.

Add half of the remaining flour mixture, and stir until combined. Stir in the remaining sour cream. Stir in the rest of the flour mixture, and then the poppy seeds.

Line a 12-cup muffin tin with paper baking cups. Fill each to the top with batter. Bake about 30 minutes, or until golden brown and a tester inserted in the center comes out clean. While the muffins are baking, mix the lemon juice and confectioners' sugar together to form a thin glaze.

Remove the muffins from the oven when ready, and allow to cool for 5 minutes. Brush the lemon glaze evenly over the top of each muffin. This is not intended to be a frosting, but just a very light glaze to give the tops a little shine and extra kiss of lemon flavor.

When cool enough to handle, remove muffins from the tins and cool completely on a rack before serving.

rhubarb crumble

Rhubarb's unique, tart flavor makes it a great complement for this easy dessert's sweet crumble topping.

serves 6

**2 pounds rhubarb
(about 6 cups cut rhubarb)**

½ cup sugar

**Grated zest and juice
of 1 orange**

**2½ cups plain or
wholewheat flour**

4 tablespoons butter

**²/₃ cup firmly packed light
brown sugar**

1 teaspoon ground ginger

Preheat oven to 375°F. Cut the rhubarb into 1-inch lengths and place in a 3-pint flameproof dish with the sugar and the orange zest and juice.

To make the crumble: Place the flour in a mixing bowl and rub in the butter with your fingertips until the mixture resembles bread crumbs. Stir in the brown sugar and the ginger.

Spread the crumble evenly over the fruit and press down lightly using a fork.

Bake in the center of the oven on a baking sheet for 25 to 30 minutes until the crumble is golden brown

Serve warm with heavy cream, ice cream, or yogurt.

cinnamon raisin bars

Here's a spicy and new-fashioned variation
on an old-fashioned oatmeal cookie.

makes 24 bars

½ **cup (1 stick) butter,
softened**

**1 cup firmly packed light
brown sugar**

1½ **cups all-purpose flour**

1 egg

1½ **cups quick-cooking
oats**

½ **teaspoon baking soda**

½ **teaspoon salt**

2 tablespoons water

For the raisin filling

¼ **cup sugar**

1 teaspoon. cinnamon

1 tablespoon cornstarch

1 cup water

2 cups raisins

Preheat oven to 350°F. In a mixing bowl, cream the butter
and brown sugar. In another bowl combine the flour, egg,
oats, baking soda, and salt; add to the creamed mixture
with the water. Beat until crumbly. Press half the oat mixture
firmly into a greased 13x9x2-inch baking pan; set the
remaining oat mixture aside.

To make the filling: In a saucepan, combine the sugar,
cinnamon, cornstarch and water until smooth; stir in raisins.
Cook and stir over medium heat until thick and bubbly. Cool
to room temperature; spread over crust. Top with reserved
oat mixture and pat down.

Bake for 30 to 35 minutes or until golden brown. Cool on
a wire rack.

For an extra sweet topping add a drizzle of icing.

index

halibut steaks with spinach and warm bacon
dressing 46
ham steaks with caramelized apples 44

ketchup: shrimp cocktail 8

lamb: grilled lamb chops with orange mint jelly 50
lemons
asparagus with lemon butter sauce 66
broiled rainbow trout with lemon parsley brown
butter 60
lemon poppy seed muffins 88
spiced-rubbed seared tuna steaks with balsamic
reduction 48
waldorf salad 18
limes
grilled salmon fillet with fresh mango salsa 42
guacamole 10
southwest corn salad 28

mangoes: grilled salmon fillet with fresh mango
salsa 42
muffins
blueberry muffins 86
lemon poppy seed muffins 88

nuts
chocolate chip cookies 80
chocolate walnut fudge 84
peanut butter cookies 82
three bean salad 20
waldorf salad 18

oyster po' boys 62

pasta
chicken fettuccini alfredo 36
deli-style macaroni salad 32
garlic shrimp angel hair 56
peanut butter cookies 82
pork: smothered pork chops 58
potatoes
perfect mashed potatoes 76
potato salad 22
roasted red potato salad 30
pumpkin: spiced pumpkin soup 16

rhubarb crumble 90

salads
caesar salad with garlic croutons 24
cobb salad 26
deli-style macaroni salad 32
potato salad 22
southwest corn salad 28
three bean salad 20
waldorf salad 18
shrimp
garlic shrimp angel hair 56
shrimp cocktail 8
soups
easy gazpacho 14
spiced pumpkin soup 16
southwest corn salad 28
spinach
baked spinach and feta frittata 48
halibut steaks with spinach and warm bacon
dressing 46
steakhouse creamed spinach 74

three bean salad 20
tomatoes
cobb salad 26
easy gazpacho 14
garlic shrimp angel hair 56
halibut steaks with spinach and warm bacon
dressing 46
succulent succotash 70
three bean salad 20
turkey cutlets 40

waldorf salad 18
walnuts
chocolate chip cookies 80
chocolate walnut fudge 84
waldorf salad 18

zucchini: succulent succotash 70